♔ Hallmark Editions

Illustrated by Norman LaLiberte
Edited by Karen Middaugh

Pathways to Happiness

Inspiration from the
World's Great Religions

PATHWAYS TO HAPPINESS

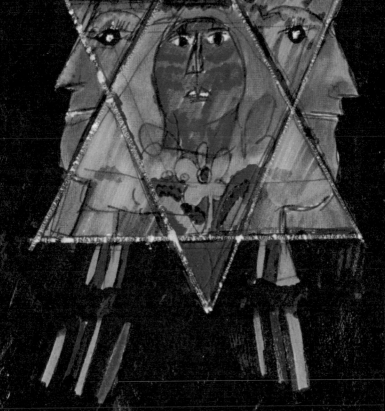

WE ARE ALL ONE

As one's life is dear to himself, so also are those of all beings. The good show compassion towards all living beings because of their resemblance to themselves.

HINDUISM

No man is an island, entire of itself; every man is a piece of the continent, a part of the main; if a clod be washed away by the sea, Europe is the less, as well as if a promontory were, as well as if a manor of thy friends or of thine own were; any man's death diminishes me, because I am involved in mankind; and therefore never send to know for whom the bell tolls; it tolls for thee.

CHRISTIANITY

As face reflects face in water,
So the mind of man reflects man.

JUDAISM

THE GREATNESS OF LOVE

Love is patient and kind; love is not jealous, or conceited, or proud; love is not ill-mannered, or selfish, or irritable; love does not keep a record of wrongs; love is not happy with evil, but is happy with the truth. Love never gives up: its faith, hope, and patience never fail.

Love is eternal. There are inspired messages, but they are temporary; there are gifts of speaking, but they will cease; there is knowledge, but it will pass. For our gifts of knowledge and of inspired messages are only partial; but when what is perfect comes, then what is partial will disappear. . . .

. . . Faith, hope, and love: . . . the greatest of these is love.

CHRISTIANITY

The nature of love is indescribable.

Like the dumb man's enjoyment of taste.

It appears in one deserving.

It is an experience without qualities, without being characterized by desire, increasing every moment, continual, and very subtle.

Obtaining it, man sees it only, hears it only, (speaks of it only), and thinks of it only.

HINDUISM

THE ART OF GIVING

One should give with faith.
One should not give without faith.
One should give with plenty.
One should give with modesty.
One should give with fear.
One should give with sympathy.

HINDUISM

Whoever shares what he has with others, must do it generously; whoever has authority, must work hard; whoever shows kindness to others, must do it cheerfully. . . . Share your belongings with your needy brothers, and open your homes to strangers.

CHRISTIANITY

The supreme path of altruism is a short-cut,
Leading to the realm of the conquerors,—
A track more speedy than that of a racing horse;
The selfish, however, know naught of it.

BUDDHISM

THE POWER OF GOODNESS

The wicked flee when no man pursues,
But the righteous are as bold as a lion.

JUDAISM

Good people shine from afar like the Himalaya mountains but the wicked are not seen, like arrows shot in the night.

BUDDHISM

Nobody lights a lamp to put it under a bowl; instead he puts it on the lamp-stand, where it gives light for everyone in the house. In the same way your light must shine before people, so that they will see the good things you do and give praise to your Father in heaven.

CHRISTIANITY

THE VIRTUOUS LIFE

Fearlessness, purity of mind, steadfastness in knowledge and concentration, charity, self-control and sacrifice, study of the scriptures, austerity, and uprightness,

Nonviolence, truth, freedom from anger, renunciation, tranquility, aversion to fault finding, compassion to living beings, freedom from covetousness, gentleness, modesty, and steadiness [absence of fickleness],

Vigour, forgiveness, fortitude, purity, freedom from malice and excessive pride—these . . . are the endowments of him who is born with the divine nature.

HINDUISM

Charity produceth the harvest in the next birth. Chastity is the parent of human happiness. Patience is an adornment becoming to all. Industry is the conductor of every personal accomplishment. Meditation is the clarifier of a beclouded mind. Intellect is the weapon which overcometh every enemy.

BUDDHISM

WORDS OF WISDOM

Although a cloth be washed a hundred times,
How can it be rendered clean and pure
If it be washed in water which is dirty?

BUDDHISM

Boast not of tomorrow;
For you know not what a day may bring forth.

JUDAISM

The wise have no doubts,
The virtuous no sorrows,
The brave no fears.

CONFUCIANISM

In this life there is none more happy than he who
has a friend to converse with, a friend to live with,
and a friend to chat with.

HINDUISM

FAITH AND ACTIONS

My brothers! What good is it for a man to say, "I have faith," if his actions do not prove it? Can that faith save him? Suppose there are brothers or sisters who need clothes and don't have enough to eat. What good is there in your saying to them, "God bless you! Keep warm and eat well!"—if you don't give them the necessities of life? This is how it is with faith: if it is alone and has no actions with it, then it is dead.

CHRISTIANITY

There is no virtue in your turning your faces towards the East or the West, but virtuous is he who believes in God, and in the Future day, and in the messenger-spirits, and the Book, and the prophets; and who gives his wealth, in spite of his love for it, to the near of kin, and the orphans, and the needy, and the wayfarer, and the beggars, and in ransoming the slaves; and who keeps up the prayers, and pays the stated alms; and those who fulfill their covenants when they covenant; and the persevering ones in hardship, and injury, and in time of war: these are the truthful, and these! they are the reverent.

ISLAMISM

THE SOURCE OF GOODNESS

A man should hasten towards the good; he should restrain his thoughts from evil. If a man is slack in doing what is good, his mind (comes to) rejoice in evil.

If a man commits sin, let him not do it again and again. Let him not set his heart on it. Sorrowful is the accumulation of evil conduct.

If a man does what is good, let him do it again and again. Let him set his heart on it. Happiness is the outcome of good conduct.

BUDDHISM

To have good fruit you must have a healthy tree; if you have a poor tree you will have bad fruit. For a tree is known by the kind of fruit it bears. You snakes—how can you say good things when you are evil? For the mouth speaks what the heart is full of. A good man brings good things out of his treasure of good things; a bad man brings bad things out of his treasure of bad things.

CHRISTIANITY

14

ON HAPPINESS IN
FAMILY LIFE

In that family, where the husband is pleased with his wife and the wife with her husband, happiness will assuredly be lasting.

HINDUISM

As my fathers planted for me, so do I plant
for my children.

Train up a child in the way he should go,
And even when he is old, he will not
depart from it.

House and wealth are an inheritance
from fathers;
But a sensible wife is a gift from the LORD.

He who loves his wife as himself, who honors her more than himself, who rears his children in the right path, and who marries them off at the proper time of their life, concerning him it is written: "And thou wilt know that thy home is at peace."

JUDAISM

DOING GOOD

He who takes part in doing good has a share therein, and he who takes part in doing evil has a burden therein; and God controls the distribution of all things.

And when you are greeted with a good greetting, then greet with a better greeting, or return the same; surely God is Accountant over all things. God is, there is no deity but He; He will most certainly gather you towards the day of the Awakening, there is no doubt therein. And who is more truthful in news than God?

ISLAMISM

Fitting hospitality must be shown even towards an enemy arrived at the house. The tree does not withdraw from the wood-cutter the shade at its side.

The good show pity even to worthless beings. The moon withholds not its light from the hovel of the outcast.

"Is this one of our tribe or a stranger?" is the calculation of the narrow-minded; but to those of a noble disposition the world itself is but one family.

HINDUISM

THE QUEST FOR TRUTH

The truth of a thing does not become greater by its frequent repetition, nor is it lessened by lack of repetition.

Let the truth and right by which you are apparently the loser be preferable to you to the falsehood and wrong by which you are apparently the gainer.

JUDAISM

They who imagine truth in untruth and see untruth in truth, never arrive at truth but follow vain imaginings (desires).

But they who know truth as truth and untruth as untruth arrive at truth and follow right desires.

BUDDHISM

. . . Nowadays nothing so completely describes . . . God as Truth. Denial of God we have known. Denial of Truth we have not known. The most ignorant among mankind have some truth in them. We are all sparks of Truth. The sum total of these sparks is indescribable, as-yet-Unknown-Truth, which is God. I am being daily led nearer to It by constant prayer.

HINDUISM

ON PRACTICING WHAT
WE PREACH

He who knoweth the precepts by heart, but fail-
eth to practice them,
Is like unto one who lighteth a lamp and then
shutteth his eyes.

BUDDHISM

Is there a wise and understanding man among
you? He is to prove it by his good life, by his good
deeds performed with humility and wisdom. But
if in your heart you are jealous, bitter, and selfish,
then you must not be proud and tell lies against
the truth. This kind of wisdom does not come
down from heaven; it belongs to the world, it is
unspiritual and demonic. For where there is jeal-
ousy and selfishness, there is also disorder and
every kind of evil. But the wisdom from above is
pure, first of all; it is also peaceful, gentle, and
friendly; it is full of compassion and produces a
harvest of good deeds; it is free from prejudice
and hypocrisy. And righteousness is the harvest
that is produced from the seeds the peacemakers
planted in peace.

CHRISTIANITY

LIVING WISELY

It is through the intellect that the human being has the capacity of honoring God.

The wise man is a greater asset to a nation than is a king.

Wisdom is the consciousness of self.

JUDAISM

The fool is tormented thinking "these sons belong to me," "this wealth belongs to me." He himself does not belong to himself. How, then, can sons be his? How can wealth be his?

The fool who knows his foolishness is wise at least to that extent; but a fool who thinks himself wise is called a fool indeed.

If a fool be associated with a wise man even all his life, he does not perceive the truth even as a spoon (does not perceive) the taste of soup.

But if a thoughtful man be associated with a wise man even for a minute, he will soon perceive the truth even as the tongue (perceives) the taste of soup.

BUDDHISM

ON MAKING WISE CHOICES

Relinquish an evil custom even though it be of thy fathers and ancestors;
Adopt a good custom even though it be established among thine enemies:
Poison is not to be taken even though offered by one's mother;
But gold is acceptable even from one who is inimical.

BUDDHISM

The good is one thing, the pleasant another; these two, having different objects, chain a man. It is well with him who clings to the good; he who chooses the pleasant, misses his end. The good and pleasant approach man: the wise goes round about them and distinguishes them. Yea, the wise prefers the good to the pleasant, but the fool chooses the pleasant through greed and avarice.

HINDUISM

THE FRUIT OF WISDOM

My son, if you receive my words,
And store my commands within you,
Inclining your ear to wisdom,
And applying your mind to reason;
If you appeal to intelligence,
And lift up your voice to reason;
If you seek her as silver,
And search for her as for hidden treasures—
Then will you understand reverence for the Lord,
And will discover the knowledge of God. . . .

For when wisdom finds a welcome within you,
And knowledge becomes a pleasure to you,
Discretion will watch over you,
Reason will guard you—
Saving you from the way of evil men.

JUDAISM

A foolish man proclaimeth his qualifications;
A wise man keepeth them secret within himself;
A straw floateth on the surface of water,
But a precious gem placed upon it sinketh.

BUDDHISM

EXAMINING OUR ACTIONS

...Whoever wishes to keep watch over himself must comply with the following two requirements. In the first place, he must know what constitutes the true good, and is therefore to be striven after, and what is unquestionably bad, and therefore to be avoided. Secondly, he must be able to classify each of his actions as either good or evil. He should do this at all times, while he is active no less than when he is quiescent. . . .

I consider it necessary for a man to conduct himself like a merchant who always takes stock of his affairs so that he may not go wrong in his reckoning. He should set aside a special time each day for the practice of self-scrutiny. For this practice, carried on not sporadically but regularly, is fraught with consequences of great import. . . .

JUDAISM

The self is the lord of self; who else could be the lord? With self well subdued a man finds a lord who is difficult to obtain.

BUDDHISM

THE WAY OF FORGIVENESS

Fair speech and forgiveness are better than charity followed by injury. For God is Rich, Forbearing. O Ye who believe! render not void your charity by show of obligation and injury, like him who spends his wealth for the sake of show of mankind, and he does not believe in God and the Future day. His attribute is as the attribute of a smooth rock with some soil thereon, then it catches a heavy rain which then leaves it a bare stone. Nothing which they earned is of any avail. For God guides not the disbelieving people.

ISLAMISM

Be helpful to one another, and forgive one another, whenever any of you has a complaint against someone else. You must forgive each other in the same way that the Lord has forgiven you.

CHRISTIANITY

SELF-CONTROL

The wise who control their body, who likewise control their speech, the wise who control their mind are indeed well controlled.

BUDDHISM

There are seven traits in a wise man:
He does not speak in the presence of one
    wiser than himself;
He does not interrupt when a colleague speaks;
He does not rush out with a rejoinder;
He asks questions that are relevant, and gives
    answers that are logical;
He deals with first things first and
    last things last;
He readily admits when he does not know
    about a matter;
He acknowledges the truth.
The opposites of these traits mark
    the boorish man.

JUDAISM

ON ACTIONS AND
THEIR EFFECTS

Unrighteousness, practiced in this world, does not at once produce its fruit, like a cow; but, advancing slowly, it cuts off the roots of him who committed it. . . .

He prospers for a while through unrighteousness, then he gains great good fortune, next he conquers his enemies, but (at last) he perishes (branch and) root.

Let him always delight in truthfulness, (obedience to) the sacred law, conduct worthy of an Aryan, and purity. . . .

HINDUISM

Fools of little understanding, being enemies to themselves, wander about doing evil deeds which bear bitter fruits.

That deed is not well done, which, having been done, brings remorse, whose reward one receives weeping and with a tearful countenance.

But that deed is well done, which, having been done, does not bring remorse, whose reward one receives delighted and happy.

BUDDHISM

THE IMPORTANCE OF
SELF-CONTROL

He who knows others is wise;
He who knows himself is enlightened.
He who conquers others has physical strength.
He who conquers himself is strong.
He who is contented is rich.
He who acts with vigor has will.
He who does not lose his place (with Tao)
      will endure.
He who dies but does not really perish
      enjoys long life.

TAOISM

If a man were to conquer in battle a thousand times a thousand men, and another conquer one, himself, he indeed is the greatest of conquerors.

He who curbs his rising anger like a chariot gone astray (over the plain), him I call a real charioteer; others but hold the reins (and do not deserve to be called charioteers).

BUDDHISM

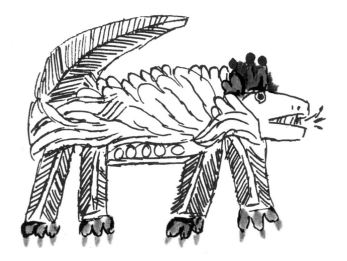

HE
WHO
CONQUERS
HiMSELF
iS
STRONG.

JUDGING OTHERS

Be humble and meek if thou would be exalted; Praise everyone's good qualities if thou would have friends.

BUDDHISM

Do not judge others, so that God will not judge you—because God will judge you in the same way you judge others, and he will apply to you the same rules you apply to others. Why, then, do you look at the speck in your brother's eye, and pay no attention to the log in your own eye? How dare you say to your brother, "Please, let me take that speck out of your eye," when you have a log in your own eye? You impostor! Take the log out of your own eye first, and then you will be able to see and take the speck out of your brother's eye.

"Do not give what is holy to dogs—they will only turn and attack you; do not throw your pearls in front of pigs—they will only trample them underfoot."

CHRISTIANITY

THE DESTRUCTIVENESS
OF HATRED

There is no sin equal to hatred and there is no penance equal to forbearance (the virtue of patience, endurance, and so on). So by all means cultivate forbearance.

Mind does not obtain peace, pleasure, or happiness, it cannot sleep or be steady so long as the bone (bit) of hate remains in the heart.

Pleasantness of my mind is not to be disturbed even when the worst evil visits me. There is nothing desirable in a bad mood of mine. Otherwise, happiness decreases.

BUDDHISM

A kindly man does good to himself;
But a cruel man does himself harm.

JUDAISM

THE MAN OF

CLEAR VISION

SOON ACQUIRES

A SERENE

COMPREHENSION

THE DISCIPLINED MIND

When a man dwells in his mind on the objects of sense, he feels an attachment for them. Attachment gives rise to desire, and desire breeds anger. From anger comes delusion, from delusion the loss of recollection, from the loss of recollection the ruin of the understanding, and from the ruin of the understanding he perishes.

But a man ot disciplined mind, who moves among the objects of sense with his senses fully under his control, and free from love and hate—he attains to a clear vision. And in that clear vision there is an end of all sorrow; for the man of clear vision soon acquires a serene comprehension. When a man has no self-control, he can have no comprehension, nor can he have the power of contemplation. And without contemplation, he can have no peace; and when he has no peace, how can he be happy? When his mind runs after the roving senses, it carries off with it the understanding, as a gale carries away a ship upon the waters.

HINDUISM

If anything is to be done, let it be done vigorously.
BUDDHISM

THE NEED FOR HUMILITY

After he had washed their feet, Jesus put his outer garment back on and returned to his place at the table. "Do you understand what I have just done to you?" he asked. "You call me Teacher and Lord, and it is right that you do so, because I am. I am your Lord and Teacher, and I have just washed your feet. You, then, should wash each other's feet. I have set an example for you, so that you will do just what I have done for you.

I tell you the truth: no slave is greater than his master; no messenger is greater than the one who sent him. Now you know this truth; how happy you will be if you put it into practice!"

CHRISTIANITY

It is through his compassionate skill in means for others that he is tied to the world,
And that, though he attained the state of a saint, yet he appears to be in the state of an ordinary person.
He has gone beyond all that is worldly, yet he has not moved out of the world;
In the world he pursues his course for the world's weal, unstained by worldly taints.

BUDDHISM

THE CHARITABLE NATURE

The highest wisdom is kindness.
Deeds of kindness are equal in weight
        to all the commandments.

Whoever gives a small coin to a poor man
has six blessings bestowed upon him, but he who
speaks a kind word to him
obtains seven blessings.

                                        JUDAISM

It is only narrow-minded men that make
        such distinctions
As "This is our friend, this our enemy";
A liberal-minded man showeth affection for all,
For it is uncertain who may yet be of aid to one....

The greatest wealth consisteth in
        being charitable,
And the greatest happiness in having
        tranquility of mind.
Experience is the most beautiful adornment;
And the best comrade is one that
        hath no desires.

                                        BUDDHISM

OUR RESPONSIBILITIES
TO SOCIETY

It is clear that, in human society, to one man's right there corresponds a duty in all other persons: the duty, namely, of acknowledging and respecting the right in question. For every fundamental human right draws its indestructible moral force from the natural law, which in granting it imposes a corresponding obligation. Those, therefore, who claim their own rights, yet altogether forget or neglect to carry out their respective duties, are people who build with one hand and destroy with the other.

CHRISTIANITY

. . . A perfected community can exist only by the perfection of its individuals, and perfection can come only by the discovery and affirmation in life by each of his own spiritual being and the discovery by all of their spiritual unity and a resultant life unity. There can be no real perfection for us except by our inner self and truth of spiritual existence taking up all truth of the instrumental existence into itself and giving to it oneness, integration, harmony.

HINDUISM

THE RULE OF LOVE

Let us live happily then, hating none in the midst of men who hate. Let us dwell free from hate among men who hate.

BUDDHISM

God is love, and whoever lives in love lives in God and God lives in him. This is the purpose of love being made perfect in us: it is that we may be full of courage on Judgment Day, because our life in this world is the same as Christ's. There is no fear in love; perfect love drives out all fear. So then, love has not been made perfect in the one who fears, because fear has to do with punishment.

We love because God first loved us. If someone says, "I love God," yet hates his brother, he is a liar. For he cannot love God, whom he has not seen, if he does not love his brother, whom he has seen. This, then, is the command that Christ gave us: he who loves God must love his brother also.

CHRISTIANITY

THE JOY OF BROTHERHOOD

Lo, how good and lovely it is
When brethren dwell together as one.
Like the goodly oil upon the head,
Which flows down upon the beard, Aaron's
      beard,
That flows down upon the edge of his robes,
So is the dew of Hermon that flows down
      upon the mountains of Zion;
For there has the LORD commanded the blessing:
Life for evermore.

JUDAISM

Return love for great hatred.
Otherwise, when a great hatred is reconciled,
      some of it will surely remain.
How can this end in goodness?
Therefore the sage holds to the left
      half of an agreement but does not exact what
      the other holder ought to do.

TAOISM

THE
BEA
OF
GO
LIFE

UT Y

A

OD

THE BEAUTY OF A
GOOD LIFE

Not the unworthy actions of others, not their (sinful) deeds of commission or omission, but one's own deeds of commission and omission should one regard.

Like a beautiful flower, full of colour but without scent, are the well-spoken but fruitless words of him who does not act (as he professes to).

But like a beautiful flower full of colour and full of scent are the well-spoken and fruitful words of him who acts (as he professes to).

As many kinds of garlands can be made from a heap of flowers, so many good works should be achieved by a mortal when once he is born.

The scent of flowers does not travel against the wind, nor that of sandalwood, nor of *tagara* and *mallika* flowers, but the fragrance of good people travels even against the wind. A good man pervades every quarter.

Sandalwood or tagara, a lotus flower or a vassiki, among these kinds of perfumes the perfume of virtue is unsurpassed.

BUDDHISM

Life is really simple, but men insist on making it complicated.

CONFUCIANISM

WISE COUNSEL
CONCERNING MEN

Do not quarrel with a powerful man,
Or you may fall into his hands.
Do not contend with a rich man,
Or he may outweigh you.
Gold has been the destruction of many,
And has perverted the minds of kings.
Do not quarrel with a garrulous man,
And do not add fuel to the fire.
Do not make sport of an uneducated man,
Or you may dishonor your own forefathers.
Do not reproach a man when he turns
     from his sin...
Do not treat a man with disrespect
     when he is old,
For all of us are growing old...
Do not neglect the discourse of wise men,
But busy yourself with their proverbs,
For from them you will gain instruction,
And learn to serve great men.

JUDAISM

It is more important that you should have a
knowledge of others, than that they should have
a knowledge of you.

CONFUCIANISM

43

THE WORTH OF WISDOM

How happy is the man who finds wisdom,
The man who gains understanding!
For her income is better than income
   of silver,
And her revenue than gold.
She is more precious than corals,
And none of your heart's desires
      can compare with her.
Long life is in her right hand,
In her left are riches and honor.
Her ways are ways of pleasantness,
And all her paths are peace.
She is the tree of life to those
   who grasp her,
And happy is every one who holds her fast.

JUDAISM

The sage has no self to call his own;
He makes the self of the people his self.
To the good I act with goodness;
To the bad I also act with goodness:
Thus goodness is attained.
To the faithful I act with faith;
To the faithless I also act with faith:
Thus faith is attained.
The sage lives in the world in concord,
      and rules over the world in simplicity.

TAOISM

ON THE NATURE OF MAN

In the Way of Heaven, there is no partiality of love; it is always on the side of the good man.

TAOISM

Good people shine from afar, like the snowy mountains; bad people are not seen like arrows shot by night.

BUDDHISM

The generous man will be enriched;
And he who waters will himself be watered.

JUDAISM

He who is really kind can never be unhappy;
He who is really wise can never be confused;
He who is really brave is never afraid.

CONFUCIANISM

THE LIFE OF CHARITY

We give this rule: the good things which we have from God ought to flow from one to another and become common to all, so that every one of us may, as it were, put on his neighbour, and so behave towards him as if he were himself in his place. They flowed and do flow from Christ to us; He put us on, and acted for us as if He Himself were what we are. From us they flow to those who have need of them; so that my faith and righteousness ought to be laid down before God as a covering and intercession for the sins of my neighbour, which I am to take on myself, and so labour and endure servitude in them, as if they were my own; for thus has Christ done for us. This is true love and the genuine truth of Christian life. But only there is it true and genuine where there is true and genuine faith. Hence the Apostle attributes to charity this quality: that she seeketh not her own.

CHRISTIANITY

Forget injuries, never forget kindnesses.

CONFUCIANISM

THE BROTHERHOOD
OF MAN

Heaven is my father and Earth is my mother, and even such a small creature as I find an intimate place in their midst.

Therefore that which fills the universe I regard as my body and that which directs the universe I consider as my nature.

All people are my brothers and sisters, and all things are my companions.

The great ruler (the emperor) is the eldest son of my parents (Heaven and Earth), and the great ministers are his stewards. Respect the aged—this is the way to treat them as elders should be treated. Show deep love toward the orphaned and the weak—this is the way to treat them as the young should be treated. The sage identifies his character with that of Heaven and Earth, and the worthy is the most outstanding man. Even those who are tired, infirm, crippled, or sick, those who have no brothers or children, wives or husbands, are all my brothers who are in distress and have no one to turn to.

CONFUCIANISM

All beings desire happiness; therefore to all extend your benevolence.

BUDDHISM

THE TREASURE OF LOVE

I have three treasures, which I hold
    and keep safe:
The first is called love;
The second is called moderation;
The third is called not venturing to go ahead
    of the world.
Being loving, one can be brave;
Being moderate, one can be ample;
Not venturing to go ahead of the world, one
     can be the chief of all officials.
Instead of love, one has only bravery;
Instead of moderation, one has only amplitude;
Instead of keeping behind, one goes ahead:
These lead to nothing but death.
For he who fights with love will win
    the battle;
He who defends with love will be secure.
Heaven will save him, and protect him
    with love.

TAOISM

Let us live happily then, hating none in the midst
of men who hate. Let us dwell free from hate
among men who hate.

BUDDHISM

RULES OF LIFE

The rule of life is to be found within yourself.

Ask yourself constantly, "What is the right thing to do?"

Beware of ever doing that which you are likely, sooner or later, to repent of having done.

It is better to live in peace than in bitterness and strife.

It is better to believe in your neighbors than to fear and distrust them.

The superior man does not wrangle. He is firm but not quarrelsome.

He is sociable but not clannish.

The superior man sets a good example to his neighbors. He is considerate of their feelings and their property.

Consideration for others is the basis of a good life, a good society.

Feel kindly toward everyone. Be friendly and pleasant among yourselves.

Be generous and fair.

CONFUCIANISM

Use no perfume but sweetness of thoughts.

BUDDHISM

THE GOLDEN RULE

Do not unto others what you would not they should do unto you.

CONFUCIANISM

Whatever you wouldst that men should not do to thee, do not do that to them. This is the whole law. The rest is only explanation.

JUDAISM

With pure thoughts and fullness of love, I will do towards others what I do for myself.

BUDDHISM

Do for others just what you want them to do for you.

CHRISTIANITY

CASTING THE FIRST STONE

[Jesus] went . . . to the Temple. The whole crowd gathered around him, and he sat down and began to teach them. The teachers of the Law and the Pharisees brought in a woman who had been caught committing adultery, and made her stand before them all. "Teacher," they said to Jesus, "this woman was caught in the very act of committing adultery. In our Law Moses gave a commandment that such a woman must be stoned to death. Now, what do you say?" They said this to trap him, so they could accuse him. But Jesus bent over and wrote on the ground with his finger. As they stood there asking questions, Jesus straightened up and said to them, "Whichever one of you has committed no sin may throw the first stone at her." Then he bent over again and wrote on the ground.

When they heard this they all left, one by one, the older ones first. Jesus was left alone, with the woman still standing there. He straightened up and said to her, "Where are they, woman? Is there no one left to condemn you?"

"No one, sir," she answered. "Well, then," Jesus said, "I do not condemn you either. You may leave, but do not sin again."

CHRISTIANITY

The true test of man's life is not his theology but his life.

JUDAISM

ON STRENGTH AND WEAKNESS

The weakest things in the world can overmatch the strongest things in the world.

Nothing in the world can be compared to water for its weak and yielding nature; yet in attacking the hard and the strong nothing proves better than it. For there is no other alternative to it.

The weak can overcome the strong and the yielding can overcome the hard.

TAOISM

A sapling whose roots have not struck deep, can be easily pulled up; but, if it be allowed to become a tree, it will be necessary to use an axe.

CONFUCIANISM

Remember this! Unless you change and become like children, you will never enter the Kingdom of Heaven. The greatest in the Kingdom of Heaven is the one who humbles himself and becomes like this child.

CHRISTIANITY

HOW TO BE HAPPY

Whoever wants to expand his field of happiness, let him rely on his moral nature.

Do good work at all times, and practice in secret meritorious deeds of all kinds.

Benefit living creatures and human beings. Cultivate goodness and happiness.

Help people in distress as you would help a fish in a dried-up rut. Free people from danger as you would free a sparrow from a fine net.

Be compassionate to orphans and kind to widows. Respect the ages and have pity on the poor.

Collect food and clothing and relieve those who are hungry and cold along the road. Give away coffins lest the dead of the poor be exposed.

If your family is well provided for, extend a helping hand to your relatives. If the harvest fails, relieve and help your neighbors and friends.

TAOISM

A contented mind is always joyful.

BUDDHISM

A CONFESSION OF FAITH

As heaven and earth are not afraid,
    and never suffer loss or harm,
Even so, my spirit, fear not thou.

As day and night are not afraid,
    nor ever suffer loss or harm,
Even so, my spirit, fear not thou.
As sun and moon are not afraid,
    nor ever suffer loss or harm,
Even so, my spirit, fear not thou.

HINDUISM

Do not be worried about the food and drink you need to stay alive, or about clothes for your body. After all, isn't life worth more than food? And isn't the body worth more than clothes? Look at the birds flying around: they do not plant seeds, gather a harvest, and put it in barns; your Father in heaven takes care of them! Aren't you worth much more than birds?

. . . Do not worry about tomorrow; it will have enough worries of its own. There is no need to add to the troubles each day brings.

CHRISTIANITY

THE MAN OF WISDOM

The wise man, by rousing himself, by vigilance, by restraint, by control, may make for himself an island which the flood cannot overwhelm.

Fools, men of inferior intelligence, fall into sloth; the wise man guards his vigilance as his best treasure.

Give not yourselves over to sloth or to the intimacy with lust and sensual pleasures. He who meditates with earnestness attains great joy.

When the wise man drives away sloth by strenuous effort climbing the high tower of wisdom, he gazes sorrowless on the sorrowing crowd below. The wise person gazes on the fools even as one on the mountain peak gazes upon the dwellers on the plain below.

BUDDHISM

I live in a very small house, but my windows look out on a very large world.

CONFUCIANISM

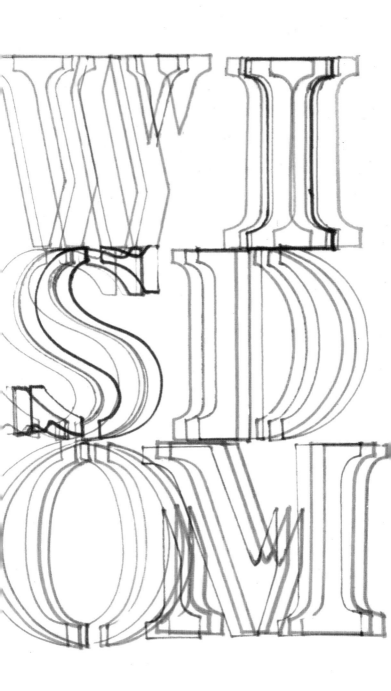

TRUE HAPPINESS

"Happy are those who know they are spiritually
      poor: the Kingdom of heaven belongs to them!
"Happy are those who mourn:
      God will comfort them!
"Happy are the meek:
      they will receive what God has promised!
"Happy are those whose greatest desire is
          to do what God requires:
      God will satisfy them fully!
"Happy are those who show mercy to others:
      God will show mercy to them!
"Happy are the pure in heart:
      they will see God!
"Happy are those who work for peace
          among men:
      God will call them his sons!
"Happy are those who suffer persecution
          because they do what God requires:
      the Kingdom of heaven belongs to them!"
                                    CHRISTIANITY

Health is the greatest of gifts, contentment the
best of riches.

                                    BUDDHISM

WHERE IS GOD?

Leave this chanting and singing and telling of beads! Whom dost thou worship in this dark corner of a temple with doors all shut?

Open thine eyes and see thy God is not before thee!

He is there where the tiller is tilling the hard ground and where the path-maker is breaking stones. He is with them in sun and in shower, and his garment is covered with dust. Put off thy holy mantle and even like him come down on the dusty soil!

Deliverance? Where is this deliverance to be found? Our master himself has joyfully taken upon him the bonds of creation; he is bound with us all forever.

Come out of thy meditations and leave aside thy flowers and incense! What harm is there if thy clothes become tattered and stained? Meet him and stand by him in toil and in the sweat of thy brow.

HINDUISM

The practice of religion involves as a first principle a loving, compassionate heart for all creatures.

BUDDHISM

. . . Let us love one another; for love comes from God; whoever loves is a child of God and knows God. Whoever does not love does not know God, because God is love. . . . If we love one another, God lives in us. . . .

CHRISTIANITY

Set in Optima, a light, open typeface designed by
Hermann Zapf which combines the grace of a
roman with the simplicity of a sans serif.
Set at the Castle Press by Grant Dahlstrom.
Printed on Hallmark Eggshell Book paper.
Designed by Claudia Becker.